Holidays Around the World

Celebrate Easter

Deborah Heiligman
Consultant, Reverend George Handzo

NATIONAL GEOGRAPHIC
WASHINGTON, D.C.

colored eggs

∧ *Painted Easter eggs*

∧ *Spring tulips*

In March or April, Christian people all over the world celebrate Easter. We celebrate with colored eggs, flowers, and prayer.

Easter is a time to celebrate the Resurrection of Jesus Christ. We celebrate the miracle of his coming back to life after death.

We also celebrate spring in all its glory. We give thanks for beautiful blooming flowers, for newborn animals, for sunshine and warm breezes.

flowers

prayer

< *Women leave an Easter Sunday church service in Ghana.*

We hear about the last days of Jesus.

Christians believe Jesus

Christ is the son of God. His story is in the part of the Bible we call the New Testament. Jesus lived about 2,000 years ago. He was a Jewish teacher, healer, and prophet. Jesus taught about love, justice, and forgiveness.

Although Easter is in the spring, some of us start getting ready for it about six weeks before. We observe Lent, which begins on Ash Wednesday. During Lent we hear about the last days of Jesus. People in power thought he was a dangerous threat, and they put him to death on a cross.

During Lent we may give up some favorite foods and some fun activities. Lent is a solemn time.

< *In the town of Boac, on Marinduque Island in the Philippines, people in an Easter procession act out the last day of Jesus.*

5

∧ *Celebrators in New Orleans enjoy Mardi Gras parades.*

Because Lent is a long, serious time, many people celebrate for days before it begins. On Shrove Tuesday, also called Fat Tuesday, we have carnivals and parties. In New Orleans there is a famous celebration called Mardi Gras, which is French for "Fat Tuesday."

> *Stilt walkers show off in Old Havana, Cuba, during Carnival.*

> Shrove Tuesday is a time for pancake races in Olney, England.

We have carnivals.

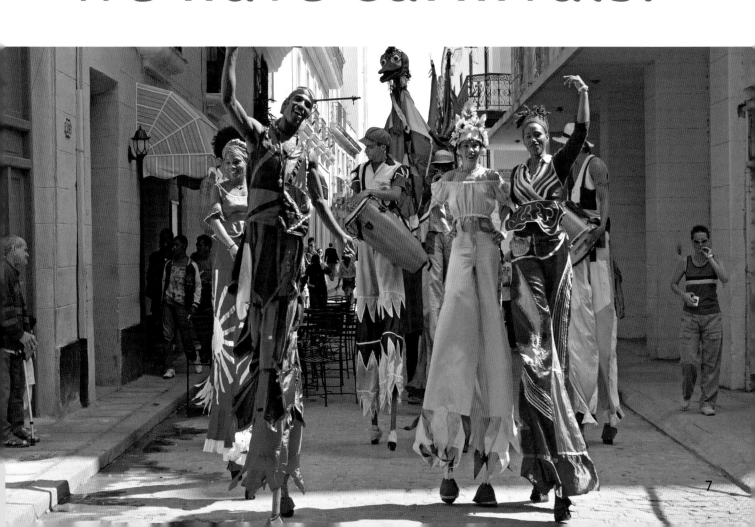

The week before Easter Sunday is called Holy Week. It starts with Palm Sunday. On Palm Sunday we have special prayer services. We hear that when Jesus rode into Jerusalem for the Passover festival, people greeted him by waving palm branches and laying them at his feet. We get palm branches at church.

We go to church

and pray.

∧ *Christians in Jerusalem, Israel,
celebrate Palm Sunday.*

< *Boys in the village of Pisac, in
Peru, pray at a church service
during Holy Week.*

On the Thursday before Easter, some
of us follow the custom of washing other
people's feet, just as Jesus washed the
feet of his followers. We also donate
money or food to those in need.

On Good Friday, we go to church and
pray. Good Friday is a sad day because
we remember how Jesus suffered as he
died on the cross.

On Easter Eve we celebrate

the light of Jesus. For many of us it is the most important celebration of the year. In many churches, people make commitments to Christianity— we have baptisms and confirmations.

We celebrate the

Sparks fly at an Easter Eve bonfire in Ratzeburg, Germany.

light of Jesus.

< *In Peremilovo, Russia, people hold candles during a church service the night before Easter.*

Easter Eve is also a time for fun. In Sweden, girls dress up as witches, knock on doors, and ask for candy and coins. Many towns in Germany have bonfires on Easter Eve. We also have Easter Eve bonfires in Texas.

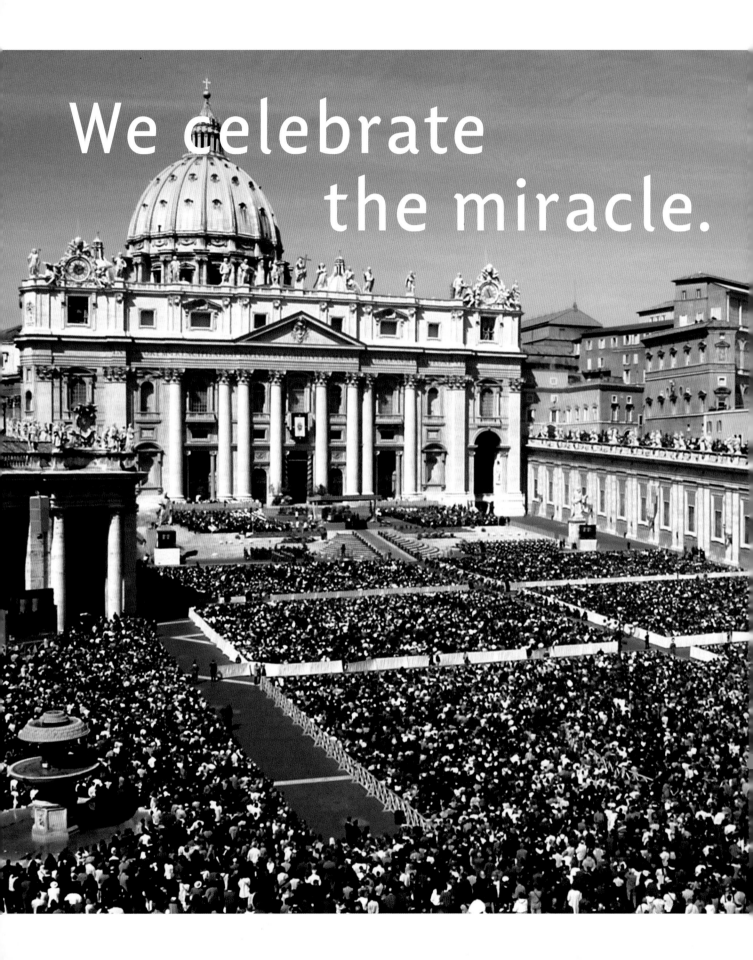

We celebrate
the miracle.

On Easter Sunday, we are

filled with joy as we celebrate the miracle of Jesus' resurrection. We hear that on the third day after Jesus died, Mary Magdalene and the other women who followed Jesus went to the cave tomb where he was buried. They were shocked to find that the rock in front of his tomb was rolled away and the tomb was empty.

In the next 40 days some people saw Jesus on Earth. Then Jesus ascended, or went up, to Heaven. His followers preached about Jesus and spread the good news. That is how the religion of Christianity began.

< *Thousands of people gather for Easter Sunday Mass every year in St. Peter's Square at the Vatican, in Rome, Italy. The leader of the Roman Catholic Church, known as the Pope, leads the service.*

We sing, "Alleluia!"

Worshippers sing together at an Easter sunrise service on the steps of the Lincoln Memorial, in Washington, D.C. The Washington Monument is in the distance.

On Easter morning some of us get up very early to go to sunrise church services. All over the world on Easter Sunday, Christians go to church to pray and sing. We sing beautiful hymns of celebration. We sing, "Alleluia!"

∧ *An Easter basket*

Easter morning brings special treats, too. Could it be the Easter Bunny was here? We get baskets of eggs—colored, decorated, and chocolate! Yummmm. In Germany, it's the Easter Hare who brings us eggs. Bunnies, chicks, and eggs are symbols of new life.

We go on Easter

egg hunts.

∧ *Everyone has fun at an Easter egg hunt in Fairfield, Connecticut.*

< *Simone Jones of Natchez, Mississippi, finds candy-filled Easter eggs in her mailbox during a neighborhood egg hunt.*

We do lots of fun things with eggs on Easter. We go on Easter egg hunts. We find eggs hidden in the grass, behind cushions, and even in the mailbox. We get to keep what we find!

< *Alberta Knight and Celia Fockler fill Easter eggs with candy and gift certificates at the Senior Center in Pullman, Washington. Children will search for more than 5,000 eggs at the city's annual egg hunt.*

Decorating eggs is a tradition that goes back a long time. We decorate eggs in many ways. We dye them, we paint them, we draw on them.

Decorating eggs

is a tradition.

We have egg rolling contests, too. Whoever gets an egg the farthest without breaking it, wins. We even have egg tapping contests. We tap each other's eggs together. If yours doesn't break you get to keep the other egg. Some of us even have egg fights!

In Greece and some other countries it is a custom to tap a friend's egg with yours and say, "Christ is risen." The friend taps back and says, "He is risen indeed."

∧ Children in Washington, D.C., enjoy themselves at the White House Easter Egg Roll, an event held every year, rain or shine.

< The Pacheco children dye eggs for their family's Easter egg hunt in Las Cruces, New Mexico.

19

We have
Easter parades.

∧ A group of friends calling themselves
the "City Chicks" march up Fifth
Avenue in New York City during the
Easter Parade.

> Jumpin' bunnies! It's a guitar
player at the Easter Parade
in Toronto, Canada.

> *Pretty in pink, Dakota the dog takes a rest on Fifth Avenue during the Easter Parade.*

Easter is a time to show off

our new spring clothes, too. We even have Easter parades! In New York City there is a parade every year. We carry Easter lilies and other flowers. Girls and women put on pretty hats called Easter bonnets. We sing the words to an old song, "In your Easter bonnet, with all the frills upon it; You'll be the grandest lady in the Easter parade."

21

"Delicious!"

A girl picks out chocolate for Easter in Damascus, Syria.

On Easter we eat lots of

delicious food. We sit down with our families for an Easter dinner. We eat roast lamb, or glazed ham, turkey, or chicken. We eat potatoes or pasta and lots of spring vegetables. We finish with yummy desserts and of course...

∧ A chocolate bunny

Easter candy! We eat lots of candy! Chocolate bunnies, cream-filled chocolate eggs, jelly beans, marshmallow chicks, and more.

∧ Jelly beans

∨ *Dylan Roden decorates very large Easter eggs at a chocolate factory in Sydney, Australia. Australians eat more chocolate Easter eggs than anyone else in the world!*

23

Easter is a time to rejoice.

Everywhere in the world Easter is

a time to rejoice and celebrate. We celebrate
the resurrection of Jesus, we celebrate spring,
we celebrate life.

*In Kona, Hawaii, people from
several churches come together
to celebrate Easter with a hula.*

MORE ABOUT EASTER

Contents

Just the Facts

WHO CELEBRATES IT: Christians

WHEN: Protestants and Roman Catholics celebrate Easter on the first Sunday following the first full moon after the spring equinox (March 21). So Easter is between March 22 and April 25. Eastern Orthodox churches (such as Greek and Ukrainian) use a different calendar, and their Easter usually comes later.

HOW LONG: Easter Sunday is one day. Lent begins about six and a half weeks before Easter. Holy Week ends on Easter Eve, which is an important night. The actual Easter season is from Easter Sunday until the Ascension (when Jesus rose to heaven) 40 days later, and then 10 more days until the feast day called Pentecost. So some Christians celebrate Easter every day for 50 days.

RITUAL: Going to church to pray and sing.

FOOD: The primary traditional foods associated with Easter are eggs, lamb, and Easter candy. Hot cross buns are a popular food usually eaten during Lent.

Easter Egg Messages

While you are decorating your Easter eggs, you might want to try something different—make an Easter egg with a message inside! To do this you will have to hollow out an egg.

WHAT YOU WILL NEED:
raw egg(s), a sewing needle, a bowl, an adult to help you.

1. Using the needle, carefully make a small hole in one end of the egg. Make a larger hole at the other end of the egg. Have an adult help you.
2. Hold the egg over a bowl. Place your mouth over the small hole, then blow hard and steady. (Do not suck in.) The insides of the egg will come out of the larger hole.
3. Rinse the hollow egg with water; let dry.
4. Decorate your egg with food coloring or markers.
5. Cut a strip of paper about 2 inches long and 1 inch wide.
6. Write a message on the strip. It can be something like "Happy Easter" or "Eat chocolate!" Or it could be a hint about where to find a treat you've hidden.
7. Fold the message and stuff it into the larger hole in the egg.
8. If you want a certain person to get this egg, put it in his or her Easter basket. Make sure the person knows he or she needs to crack open the egg to get the message.

We Sing with Joy: Hymns for Easter

Singing is a big part of Easter celebrations. Here are two hymns often sung at Eastertime.

THE EXSULTET

The "Exsultet" was written about 1,500 years ago. It is sung during the Easter Vigil, held the night before Easter Sunday. The church is dark, and the deacon comes in holding the Paschal candle. The candle's flame represents the light of Jesus. The "Exsultet" is very long. Here is part of it:

Rejoice now, heavenly hosts and choirs of angels, and let your trumpets shout Salvation for the victory of our mighty King...

Rejoice and sing now, all the round earth, bright with a glorious splendor, for darkness has been vanquished by our eternal King...

Rejoice and be glad now, Mother Church, and let your holy courts, in radiant light, resound with the praises of your people...

This is the night, when Christ broke the bonds of death and hell, and rose victorious from the grave...

Holy Father, accept our evening sacrifice, the offering of this candle in your honor. May it shine continually to drive away all darkness. May Christ, the Morning Star who knows no setting, find it ever burning—he who gives his light to all creation, and who lives and reigns for ever and ever. Amen.

∧ Chinese Catholics sing during an Easter service in Beijing, China.

THE PASCHAL TROPARION

People in the Eastern Orthodox tradition sing this hymn during the Easter Vigil and throughout the Easter season. It comes from the very beginnings of Christianity and is found in all the languages of the Eastern Church (such as Greek and Russian).

Christ is risen from the dead,
Trampling down death by death,
And upon those in the tombs
Bestowing life!

Franny's Tatales

My friend Elvira Woodruff says Easter is not Easter without the Italian Easter cookies called *tatales*. This recipe is from her mother, Franny Pirozzi.

Makes about 5 dozen cookies.

INGREDIENTS:
4 cups all-purpose flour, plus another cup or so for flouring your hands
4 teaspoons baking powder
3/4 cup sugar
1/2 teaspoon salt
6 eggs, beaten well
1 cup (2 sticks) butter, melted
4 teaspoons vanilla extract
Round multicolored sprinkles (nonpareils)

FOR THE ICING:
2 to 4 tablespoons milk
1 cup confectioner's sugar

1. In a large bowl, mix together the flour, baking powder, sugar, and salt.

2. Make a well in the center of the flour mixture and add the eggs, melted butter, and vanilla. Mix well. You can do this with an electric mixer. If the dough gets too thick for the mixer, finish mixing it with a spoon.

3. Preheat the oven to 350° F.

4. Flour your hands: Put the extra cup of flour in a shallow plate, then gently pat your palms in the flour so that flour sticks to them.

5. Using your floury hands, form the dough into small round balls and place them about 1 inch apart on an ungreased cookie sheet. You will need to keep flouring your hands often to keep the dough from sticking to them!

6. Bake the cookies for 8 to 10 minutes, or until the bottoms are light brown.

7. While the cookies bake, make the icing: Add enough of the milk to the confectioners sugar to form a thick paste.

8. Spread the icing over the warm cookies and sprinkle with multicolored sprinkles.

9. Once the cookies have completely cooled, you will probably eat them all up. But if you don't, store them in an airtight container.

Learn More

BOOKS

Those with a star (*) are especially good for children.

*Fisher, Aileen. *The Story of Easter.* HarperCollins, 1997. A very simple retelling of the story of Easter as well as good information about Easter customs.

*Knudsen, Shannon. *Easter Around the World.* Carolrhoda Books, 2005. A tour of Easter customs around the world.

MacDonald, Margaret Read, editor. *The Folklore of World Holidays.* Gale, 1992. This is a book that you can find in your library. It is a good reference book for many world holidays.

Spirin, Gennady. *The Easter Story According to the Gospels of Matthew, Luke & John from the King James Bible.* Henry Holt, 1999. This is a book meant for children, but it would be best understood read with an adult. The words are from the New Testament, and the paintings are by a wonderful artist, Gennady Spirin.

WEB SITES

www.easterbilby.com.au/
Learn all about the bilby and the campaign to replace the Easter Bunny with the Easter Bilby—in Australia.

allcrafts.net/easter.htm
This site has links to many Easter crafts and tips on how to decorate eggs. They are free, but you do have to put up with advertisements.

gardenersnet.com/flower/easterlily.htm
You might get an Easter lily as a present, or give one to your mom. If you want to try to keep it alive for years, visit this Web site.

EDUCATIONAL EXTENSIONS

Reading

1. How is the spring season relevant to celebrating the miracle of Jesus's resurrection?

2. There are many important days leading up to Easter Sunday such as Shrove/Fat Tuesday, Palm Sunday, and Good Friday. Can you describe some of the traditions that occur on one of these days and explain why they take place?

3. Pick a favorite photograph from the text and reread its caption. What symbols of Easter can you see in the photo? (Hint: Expand upon the information given and the details observed in relation to the context of the page.)

4. Conduct a short research project on the Easter traditions of a country, culture, or community of your choice. Use at least 3 print or digital sources to gather information. (Hint: If you're having trouble choosing what to study, use the map on page 30 for ideas.)

5. In pairs, report on your Easter research topic. Tell your partner what you discovered, what facts interested you most, and what sources you used. After everyone has finished discussing, share what information you learned from your partner's research project.

V *In Sacramento, California, Stefani Sacchetti and Mireille Gutierrez giggle as they crack each other over the head with hollowed-out eggs filled with confetti—a Latino Easter tradition.*

Glossary

Ash Wednesday: The first day of Lent for Western Christians. Roman Catholics and other Christians receive a cross made of ashes on their foreheads. The ashes are made by burning dried palms from last year's Palm Sunday.

Baptism: A ceremony in which a person, usually a baby, is sprinkled with or dunked in water to become part of the Christian faith.

Christian/Christianity: Christians are those who practice Christianity, the religion that is based on the belief that Jesus Christ is the Son of God and the Messiah, or savior. There are different branches of Christianity, including various Protestant denominations (such as Baptists and Lutherans), as well as Catholics (Roman Catholics and Eastern Orthodox).

Confirmation: A ceremony in which a person affirms Christian belief.

Disciple (duh-SYE-puhl): A follower. There were 12 disciples who were closest to Jesus Christ.

Paschal (PAHS-kul): An adjective meaning Easter.

Tomb (toom): A room or building for holding a dead body. In ancient times people were often buried in caves. Often a rock was put in front to prevent grave-robbing.

Where This Book's Photos Were Taken

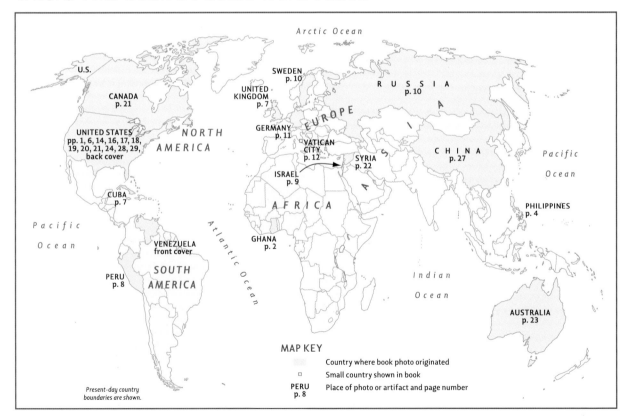

Arctic Ocean

U.S.

CANADA
p. 21

UNITED STATES
pp. 1, 6, 14, 16, 17, 18,
19, 20, 21, 24, 28, 29,
back cover

NORTH
AMERICA

SWEDEN
p. 10

UNITED
KINGDOM
p. 7

GERMANY
p. 11

EUROPE

VATICAN
CITY
p. 12

RUSSIA
p. 10

CHINA
p. 27

Pacific

Ocean

SYRIA
p. 22

ISRAEL
p. 9

CUBA
p. 7

AFRICA

Pacific

Ocean

VENEZUELA
front cover

SOUTH
AMERICA

GHANA
p. 2

Atlantic Ocean

PERU
p. 8

PHILIPPINES
p. 4

Indian

Ocean

AUSTRALIA
p. 23

MAP KEY

Country where book photo originated

Small country shown in book

PERU
p. 8   Place of photo or artifact and page number

Present-day country boundaries are shown.

Easter: A Celebration of New and Enduring Life

by Reverend George Handzo

For Christians, Easter is the holiest and most important event in the year—even more important than Christmas. The essence of Easter is the celebration of the resurrection of Jesus Christ from the dead. In this event, we remember how God allowed his son to die so that he could be resurrected. We believe that this resurrection atones for all of our sins and overcomes death. Through Jesus' death and resurrection we are given eternal life with God in heaven.

Jesus was a Jew. He lived according to Jewish law and custom. So it was that, as a good Jew, he came to Jerusalem to celebrate the Passover festival. He was greeted by a crowd of people who waved palm branches at him and shouted blessings to him, because many believed he was a prophet or a king who had come to liberate them from the Romans. Through long custom, we burn the leftover palms to make the ashes for the next year's Ash Wednesday, which marks the beginning of Lent.

Jesus' last celebration of the Passover became known as the Last Supper, now celebrated as Holy Communion, or the Eucharist. The fact that Jesus was crucified as the Jewish Sabbath was approaching dictated both the speed with which Joseph of Arimathea had to bury him and the fact that no one went to visit the tomb until two days later, when the Sabbath was over.

In the first few centuries after Christ, the season of Lent between Ash Wednesday and Easter was the time when those who were preparing to become Christians underwent their final preparation for baptism through intense study, fasting, and denial of normal pleasures. Baptism only happened once a year—just before Easter morning. The baptisms represented a rising to new life along with Jesus.

All religious traditions have been created by adding something new, while borrowing from the traditions that preceded them. Thus Christianity was influenced by Judaism, and both were influenced by pagan traditions that came before them.

Like many other religious holidays, Easter is a mixture of several influences that have been blended together over many years to create the occasion we know today. For instance, some scholars believe that the name Easter comes from Eastre, an ancient goddess of spring and fertility whose festival was celebrated around what is now the month of April. Likewise, the rabbit and eggs are associated with fertility. These ancient traditions complement the emphasis on new life represented in the story of the resurrection. However, as with Christmas, many people celebrate the cultural aspects of the holiday and neglect the religious part of the celebration.

Finally, each culture and ethnic group that celebrates Easter has contributed its own particular customs and foods to the holiday. In the Slovak part of my family, for example, the special dish for Easter Sunday was goose. In the German part of my family, it was ham.

While the particular Easter traditions may differ and come from various influences, they all contribute to a holiday based around the celebration of new and enduring life.

Reverend George Handzo is an Associate Vice President of the HealthCare Chaplaincy, an international center for pastoral care, education, and research. It is based in New York.

For Marfé Ferguson Delano and Lori Epstein, with undying gratitude.

PICTURE CREDITS

Page 1: © Tina Fineberg/Associated Press; page 2: © Tim Beddow/ Eye Ubiquitous/ Hutchison; page 3 (top): © Photodisc; page 3 (bottom): © Andreea Manciu/ Shutterstock; pages 4-5: © Mark Downey/ Lucid Images; page 6: © Ted Soqui/Corbis; page 7 (top): © Matt Dunham/ Associated Press; page 7 (bottom): © Jose Fuste Raga/Corbis; page 8: © Werner Bischof/ Magnum Photos; page 9: © Hanan Isachar; page 10 (top): © Lena Johansson/ Getty Images; page 10 (bottom): © Alexander Zemlianichenko/ Associated Press; page 11: © Michael Probst/ Associated Press; pages 12-13: © Massimo Sambucetti/ Associated Press; pages 14-15: © J. Scott Applewhite/ Associated Press; page 16 (top): © Photodisc; page 16 (bottom): © Ben Hillyer/ The Natchez Democrat/ Associated Press; page 17: © Joel Sartore/ National Geographic Image Collection; page 18 (top): © Moscow-Pullman Daily News/ Associated Press; page 18 (bottom): © Norm Dettlaff/ Las Cruces Sun-News/ Associated Press; page 19: © Robert Trippett/WpN; page 20: © Stephen Chernin/Getty Images; page 21 (top): © Jeff Christensen JC/HB/ Reuters; page 21 (bottom): © Tony Bock/Toronto Star/ZUMA Press; page 22: © BassemTellawi/ Associated Press; page 23 (top): © Eileen Meyer/ Shutterstock; page 23 (center): © Gavin MacVicar/ Shutterstock; page 23 (bottom): © David Gray/ Reuters; pages 24-25: © Bob Brown Eye Expression Photography; page 27: © Elizabeth Dalziel/ Associated Press; page 28: © Marfe Ferguson Delano; page 29: © Chriss Crewell/ ZUMA; Front cover: Patricia Vazquez/SuperStock; Back cover: Jeff Christensen/Reuters; Spine: Brand X.

Text copyright © 2007 Deborah Heiligman
Compilation copyright © 2007 National Geographic Society
Reprinted in paperback and library binding, 2016

Published by the National Geographic Society.
All rights reserved. Reproduction of the whole or any part of the contents without written permission from the publisher is prohibited.

The Library of Congress catalogued the 2007 edition as follows:
Heiligman, Deborah.
  Celebrate Easter with colored eggs, flowers, and prayer /
Deborah Heiligman ; consultant, George Handzo.
    p. cm. -- (Holidays around the world)
  ISBN-13: 978-1-4263-0020-2 (hardcover)
  ISBN-13: 978-1-4263-0021-9 (library binding)
  1. Easter--Juvenile literature. I. Handzo, George. II. Title.
BV55.H45 2007
263'.93--dc22
                    2006026224

2016 paperback edition ISBN: 978-1-4263-2370-6
2016 reinforced library binding ISBN: 978-1-4263-2371-3

National Geographic supports K–12 educators with ELA Common Core Resources. Visit natgeoed.org/commoncore for more information.

Front cover: A baby rabbit sniffs wildflowers on a warm spring day.
Back cover: A Saint Bernard displays her Easter best, including a bonnet and pastel nails.
Title page: Ten-year-old Robin Lucas and her great-grandmother Doris Watlington smile for the camera at the Easter parade in New York City.

Printed in Hong Kong
15/THK/1

The National Geographic Society is one of the world's largest nonprofit scientific and educational organizations. Founded in 1888 to "increase and diffuse geographic knowledge," the Society's mission is to inspire people to care about the planet. It reaches more than 400 million people worldwide each month through its official journal, *National Geographic*, and other magazines; National Geographic Channel; television documentaries; music; radio; films; books; DVDs; maps; exhibitions; live events; school publishing programs; interactive media; and merchandise. National Geographic has funded more than 10,000 scientific research, conservation, and exploration projects and supports an education program promoting geographic literacy.

For more information, please visit nationalgeographic.com, call 1-800-NGS LINE (647-5463), or write to the following address:
National Geographic Society, 1145 17th Street N.W., Washington, D.C. 20036-4688 U.S.A.

Visit us online at nationalgeographic.com/books
For librarians and teachers: ngchildrensbooks.org
More for kids from National Geographic: kids.nationalgeographic.com

For information about special discounts for bulk purchases, please contact National Geographic Books Special Sales: ngspecsales@ngs.org

For rights or permissions inquiries, please contact National Geographic Books Subsidiary Rights: ngbookrights@ngs.org

STAFF FOR THIS BOOK

Nancy Laties Feresten, Vice President, Editor-in-Chief of Children's Books
Bea Jackson, Design and Illustrations Director, Children's Books
Amy Shields, Executive Editor, Children's Books
Marfé Ferguson Delano, Project Editor
Lori Epstein, Senior Photo Editor
Melissa Brown, Project Designer
Callie Broaddus, Associate Designer
Carl Mehler, Director of Maps
Priyanka Lamichhane, Assistant Editor
Rebecca Baines, Editorial Assistant
Paige Towler, Editorial Assistant
R. Gary Colbert, Production Director
Lewis R. Bassford, Production Manager
Vincent P. Ryan, Maryclare Tracy, Nicole Elliott, Manufacturing Managers
Kelsey Carlson, Education Consultant

Series design by 3+Co. and Jim Hiscott.
The body text in the book is set in Mrs. Eaves.
The display text is Lisboa.

ACKNOWLEDGMENTS

Many, many thanks to Father Nathan Humphrey, who gave this book and me a lot of time and great advice and also to Reverend Nadine Hundertmark for her insight and input. Thanks to Anne Stone and Celia Hartmann, too. Many people offered advice and recipes, but a special thanks goes to Elvira Woodruff for giving us her mother Franny's delicious cookie recipe. And thanks to Marfé Ferguson Delano for, among other things, making a batch and taking the great photo. Thanks to Lori Epstein, as always, for finding the most beautiful photos the world over. Thanks to Julie Stockler for suggesting some great Easter activities. Easter brings back many childhood memories for me, not because I celebrated it, but because I didn't. Thanks to my next-door neighbors in Allentown, PA, the Riegels, for sharing your jelly beans and chocolate bunnies every Easter. Sorry if I begged.